LADY GAGA TO Z

A CELEBRATION OF A POP CULTURE ICON

Written by Satu Hämeenaho-Fox
Illustrated by Nastka Drabot

INTRODUCTION

There are so many Lady Gagas. There's the ultimate electro-pop superstar, committed to cranking out big hits and entertaining us with incredible spectacle. There's the jazz musician, collaborating with the legendary singer Tony Bennett. There's the actor, transforming herself into what the story needs. There's the artist, creating incredible, thoughtful visuals through videos and fashion. Last, but definitely not least, there's Gaga the person, who and pours her heart out in her music and lyrics and wants to make the world a kinder and fairer place.

Her passion for LGBTQ+ equality is a huge part of her story: her mission to "inject gay culture into the mainstream" has rightly earned her the status of a queer icon. Her Born This Way Foundation has been supporting young people's mental health for over a decade and she has bravely faced backlash and hate for her convictions throughout her career.

Whether you got into Gaga during her dirty pop phase or fell for her warmth and heart as Ally in the movie *A Star Is Born*, this book will take you through all the key moments of Gaga's career. We'll trace her fashion evolution from hair bows to haute couture, and shine a spotlight on some of her most eye-catching looks. We'll take a dive into her discography, from her iconic pop beginnings with *The Fame* to her more stripped-back approach on *Joanne*. And we'll look at some of her most groundbreaking collaborations, from Bradley Cooper and Beyoncé to Blackpink and Ariana Grande.

What matters most to Gaga is self-expression and being yourself, as illustrated in her most enduring song "Born This Way." Instantly a groundbreaking anthem of self-acceptance, the song acts as something of a manifesto of everything Gaga stands for: love, respect, empathy, and the pure power of pop. Unleash your inner Little Monster: here is the remarkable story of the unique life, and talent, of Lady Gaga.

DISCLAIMER
This book has not been written or endorsed by Lady Gaga. It was created for Little Monsters, by Little Monsters. It is a love letter to Lady Gaga and all those who feel connected to her.

3

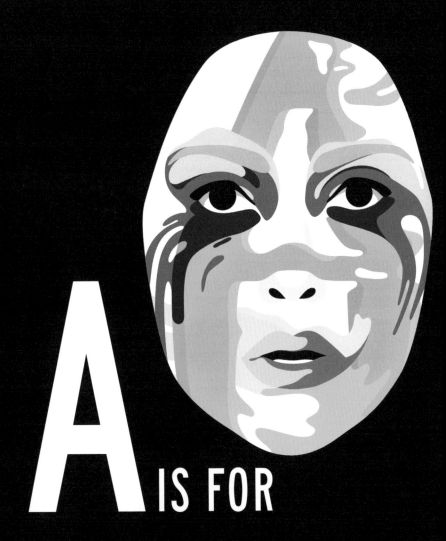

A IS FOR

ARTPOP

Instead of becoming more radio-friendly or debuting a "sexy new look" for her third album, Gaga drew on her art-school training to create the 2013 masterpiece *Artpop*. The album opens with a reference to Marxist art-critic Walter Benjamin's theory of the "aura" of art.

The lead single was "Applause," a massive electro tune about how Gaga's fans saved her. She said that when she was in a dark place after an injury: "...it was the applause that kept me going. Every night when I went on stage it was the cheering of the fans and it was their smiling faces and all the glitter and the leather and the costumes and their passion [that] kept me alive." In the video, Gaga appears as Botticelli's Venus, and holds a prosthetic leg above her head to represent her own broken hip.

Critical reception was mixed, with some people saying it wasn't as adventurous as Gaga's previous albums. As cultural commentator Mike's Mic responded, "*Artpop* doesn't sound experimental? It sounds boring? It sounds normal? Did you even listen to it?" *Artpop* was simply ahead of its time.

A IS ALSO FOR...

AMERICAN IDOL

Gaga first appeared on the long-running talent show *American Idol* in 2009, playing "Poker Face" on a piano filled with bubbles. In 2011, she mentored the four finalists, saying, "I'm not interested in judging them, I'm here purely to be a friend," before asking if the contestants were willing to get "a little psycho?" After she encouraged conservative Christian singer Scotty McCreery to treat the microphone like his girlfriend, he said: "I knew going into it it would be interesting, I just wasn't prepared for how interesting it was," before kissing his cross as protection.

ARMADILLO BOOTS

The most memorable Gaga shoes have to be the Alexander McQueen "armadillo" boots she wore in the video for "Bad Romance." The curved, teetering heels made her look like a crab-like creature, and are a symbol of peak Weird Gaga. When three pairs of the limited edition of only 21 were sold at auction, in 2015, Gaga snapped them up with her crab claws, saying, "there is no diamond, no award, nothing I ever wanted more than a memory of my brief friendship with McQueen."

ADAM DRIVER

Gaga's *House of Gucci* co-star Adam Driver is kind of her male equivalent, without the singing: an intense, committed actor who she affectionately calls "a weirdo like me." Their natural chemistry made even the sex scene easy to shoot. Driver says, "we blocked it out as we would any fight or any scene, then we just kind of ran it maybe once or twice, and that was it!" He went on to add, "we were feeling it, so to speak!" As for a future Oscar win for Gaga, he said he'll be "waiting in the wings" ready to go out and celebrate her.

ALLY MAINE

Gaga has played many characters, but Ally from *A Star Is Born* is the one that changed how we see her forever. Ally looks like a normal girl: she's nervous about performing and has to be nudged into the spotlight, which is very different to Gaga's own hustle and determination. As Gaga says, "the character of Ally is informed by my life experience. But I also wanted to make sure that she was not me." In embodying Ally, Gaga proved she is an incredible actor and that her talent can shine without elaborate costumes or stagecraft.

AMERICAN HORROR STORY: HOTEL

The long-running *American Horror Story* series is the extremely grisly brainchild of director Ryan Murphy. He cast Gaga as the Countess in the fifth series, *Hotel*. It's not a spoiler to say that she's a vampire who exerts control over her many lovers and minions. Gaga looks incredible in period costumes from the 1920s to the present day, bringing full undead glamour to many, many sexy montages.

A IS ALSO FOR...

ARTS & HUMANITIES COMMITTEE

When Joe Biden became US president in 2021, he reinstated a committee that advises the White House on how to promote art and culture (the whole committee had resigned in protest under Donald Trump's presidency). Lady Gaga was appointed the co-chair of the committee in 2023, and works alongside George Clooney and Shonda Rhimes among many behind-the-scenes people from the world of art and entertainment.

IS FOR

BORN THIS WAY

Lady Gaga's second album *Born This Way* sounds good in the club, but underneath the basslines it is an earnest statement about equality and identity. The title track was politically radical for its time, and is still unique in how frankly it expresses its support for minorities. This is not a bland "love is love" message, but a direct statement that people who are gay, lesbian, bisexual, and trans, as well as people of colour and disabled people, are worthy of both celebration and support.

Born This Way is also at least as much about the dark glitter of nightlife. "Government Hooker" is a jaw-dropping song based on the title alone, while "Marry the Night" is Gaga saying if she can't have love, she may as well dedicate herself to going out. There are a lot of religious references on the album, from the song "Black Jesus" to the gospel sound of "Fashion of His Love," but anyone is welcome to join Gaga in her "Electric Chapel." Whether you think of the chapel as a church, the club, or some other safe space is up to you.

BRAVERY

Gaga often speaks about bravery, whether it's her own or the bravery of other people she loves, from her fans to the LGBTQ+ community. Gaga's core message is to have the bravery to be authentically yourself, even if—especially if—other people don't like it. Yet, when she played Madison Square Garden in 2011, she told the crowd that she wasn't born this way, "I didn't used to be brave. In fact I wasn't very brave at all. But you have made me brave, Little Monsters."

BUBBLE DRESS

Gaga already had a bubble-filled piano, now she needed a bubbly outfit to go with it. Her nude bodysuit covered in a dress of plastic bubbles was hand-crafted by Haus of Gaga. Although in reality it is priceless, when she wore the bespoke look in a sketch on *Saturday Night Live*, she said it cost $20,000. In the sketch, Andy Samberg has embarrassingly shown up in an identical look and says his is made of garbage. "Fashion!" they giggle The bubble dress should not be confused with Gaga's bubble-blowing dress, a white dress with 3D-printed fans that blow bubbles.

B IS ALSO FOR...

"BAD ROMANCE"

Probably Gaga's most famous song after "Shallow" and definitely the signature song of the weirder Gaga eras, "Bad Romance" has it all. The stuttering, repeated nonsense words are here ("rah, rah-ah-ah-ah"), the references to herself ("Gaga, ooh-la-la!"), and the love story gone wrong. It could also read as an invitation to Little Monsters to join the fandom, because it says you can be ugly, diseased, "psycho," or a criminal, and Gaga will still want you. Truly, there's a place for all of us in the church of Mother Monster.

B IS ALSO FOR...

BRADLEY COOPER

The creative force behind 2018 movie *A Star Is Born* is more than just an actor, writer, singer, and director to Gaga: Bradley Cooper is the person who gave her the role of a lifetime and changed her career in the process. Their impassioned duet of "Shallow" at the 2019 Oscars ceremony made some people believe they'd fallen in love, while playing Ally and Jackson Maine. Given they were both nominated for Oscars that year, we have to assume they are just very good at acting.

BRANDON MAXWELL

Designer and stylist Brandon Maxwell was Gaga's fashion director between 2012 and 2018, and still dresses her to this day. She has worn his (very expensive) line on the red carpet, especially to more formal events such as the Royal Variety Performance, where she wore a polished silver gown with a high neck. Gaga wore Brandon Maxwell to the 2019 Met Gala, or rather she wore four Brandon Maxwells! The designer was on hand to remove her huge pink overcoat, black evening dress, and slim pink gown, until Gaga was stripped down to her underwear.

BLACKPINK

"Sour Candy" from 2020 album *Chromatica* was a collaboration between Gaga and K-pop girlband Blackpink. Gaga's growl pairs well with Lisa, Jisoo, Jennie, and Rosé's smooth voices, but unfortunately, due to the Covid-19 pandemic, there was no chance of bringing the five of them together for a performance. The concept is the best aspect of the song because it reveals something about Gaga: she is hard and sour on the outside, a tough nut to crack, but once you get to know her, she's actually really sweet.

IS FOR

CHROMATICA

At first it seemed that the delayed release of *Chromatica*, Gaga's sixth album, was a bad thing. No one knew what to expect after the Tony Bennett collaborations, *Joanne*, and *A Star Is Born* took her on a very different trajectory to her earlier career.

But the timing turned out to be a defining feature of how this record impacted our lives. We should have known that the dancefloor would always call to Gaga. Right in the middle of the least social era of everyone's lives, she finally dropped Lady Gaga 6 in May 2020 and turned our living rooms into clubs.

The first single "Stupid Love" set the tone, and then the all-conquering "Rain on Me" arrived. The song is a duet with Ariana Grande, whose light, super-high voice is the perfect companion to Gaga's lower, growling vocals. It became one of the defining songs of 2020 – a very short playlist given how few artists dared to release anything during the first year of the pandemic.

C IS ALSO FOR...

CHROMATICA BALL

Arriving at the Chromatica live tour after a two-year delay was a special moment for both Gaga and the fans. The show was as spectacular as ever, and marked her first tour that was all stadiums rather than a mix of bigger and smaller venues, showing how many new fans she had gained since the Joanne tour of 2017. The costumes included a stone-look sarcophagus that split open to reveal a shoulder-padded catsuit.

CATHOLIC SCHOOL

Gaga attended a private, all-girls Catholic School in New York, called Convent of the Sacred Heart, where Paris Hilton was also once a student. The uniform of a grey tunic, with shorts underneath for modesty reasons, was not to Gaga's taste. Returning in 2010 for a performance to mark her younger sister Natali's graduation from the school, she wore sky-high heels and a beekeeper's hat.

CHEEK TO CHEEK

Legendary singer-songwriter Tony Bennett is 59 years older than Lady Gaga, but they found musical ground in common for their 2014 collaborative album. A huge surprise after three albums of pure pop, Gaga decided it was time to be respected for her voice as well as her radio-friendly tunes and shock-tactic outfit choices. *Cheek to Cheek* got rave reviews for the pair's gorgeous singing, and they played 36 live shows together.

CHER

Gaga has often been compared to Cher. They have both had careers in music and acting, and share a maximalist approach to fashion. Gaga even wrote Cher a potential duet called "The Greatest Thing". Gaga said "Cher heard the song and loved it and wanted to do it together. And I said, 'F*** yeah, it's Cher!'" Sadly due to problems with production, the song never saw the light of day and remains a mystery track.

CARPOOL KARAOKE

TV host James Corden drove Gaga around LA for a karaoke session in 2016, the *Joanne* era. Gaga's vocals nearly took the roof off the car as she sang the first single from the album, "Perfect Illusion" and donned the pink hat from the album cover. A big reveal was that Gaga had just passed her driving test — she took the wheel for a slightly bumpy ride.

CHRISTIAN CARINO

Gaga dated talent agent Christian Carino for two years between 2017 and 2019. He is an industry player in his own right, representing artists like J-Lo, Harry Styles and Margot Robbie at the huge agency CAA. Imagine the gossip they knew between them! Christian and Gaga got engaged, but by Februar 2019 it was over.

C IS ALSO FOR...
COACHELLA

Stepping in after Beyoncé got pregnant, Gaga headlined the Coachella festival in 2017. She went against expectations by remixing the ballad "A Million Reasons" as a club banger, but then slowing down "Edge of Glory" to a piano-led version. Gaga was due to play again in 2020, but wasn't able to make the rescheduled date after postponement because of Covid-19.

IS FOR

DOGS

Gaga has three French bulldogs called Koji, Gustav, and Miss Asia. Her constant companions in life, through lockdown and international travel, Miss Asia even appeared with Gaga on the cover of *Harper's Bazaar* magazine. It seems like a cushy life for the pups. But one day, in February 2021, Gaga's dog walker and "nanny to a frenzy of Frenchies," Ryan Fischer, took them out for walkies. Suddenly, he was rushed by three strangers and shot with a semi-automatic handgun. Miss Asia ran away in panic, and the stranger grabbed Koji and Gustav and ran off, leaving Ryan bleeding and screaming for help.

Gaga was devastated and announced she would pay $500,000 for the return of her dogs, "no questions asked." The dogs were returned, but in a shocking twist the woman who brought them back turned out to be involved in the crime, and later had the audacity to sue Gaga for the reward. Happily, Ryan survived the shooting.

D IS ALSO FOR...

DRAG RACE

Gaga and Drag Race is an obvious match made in heaven. For her appearance on the season 9 premiere in 2017, Gaga pranked the queens by pretending to be "Ronnie, New Jersey's number one Lady Gaga impersonator." The contestants were feeling the pressure at her spot-on impersonation until it finally began to dawn on them that this was the actual Lady Gaga herself.

DIVE BAR TOUR

The rootsy sound of Gaga's album *Joanne* called for a different kind of tour. In a move possibly inspired by the bar where we meet her character in the 2018 movie *A Star Is Born*, Gaga sang in dive bars in Nashville, New York, and LA. The crowd was made up of just 300 or so handpicked fans, who were treated to a much more intimate experience than the usual stadium show: Gaga even crowdsurfed!

DADA WILLIAMS

Matthew "Dada" Williams was part of Gaga's creative team and the creative director of Haus of Gaga from 2008 to 2010. He and Gaga also had a passionate romantic relationship. Gaga said, "Dada is quite brilliant and we were crazy lovers, but I stopped it when we discovered what a strong creative connection we had." They seem to remain on good terms, with Dada posting images of Gaga in one of his designs for Givenchy, where he is now the artistic director.

IS FOR

THE EGG

The 2011 Grammys were proceeding as normal: Rihanna and Katy Perry arrived looking gorgeous, and the red carpet seemed like it was off to it's usual, elegant start. Suddenly, a flurry of security and photographers shuffled onto the carpet, and behind them were sculpted models carrying what looked like a huge, gummy, sinister alien egg. Inside, you could just see a person wearing black gloves pressing their hands against the side of the casing. There was only one person this could possibly be, but she didn't reveal herself.

Inside, on the main stage, the latex egg appeared again, lit from inside. Gaga was finally revealed, wearing prosthetic shoulders that made her look like an extra-terrestrial, possibly from the 1980s. She sang "Born This Way" and as Gaga put it, "I really wanted to be born onstage." The egg clearly represented that some of us are just born different.

She later revealed to *Vanity Fair* that she had been in the egg for three days beforehand to be ready for her performance–that's some impressive commitment!

E IS ALSO FOR...

ELTON JOHN

As two of pop's most flamboyant stars, it's not surprising that Gaga and Elton John hit it off. Elton famously has a great eye for new talent and he proved it when he joined Gaga onstage at the 2010 Grammys and jumped on "Sine From Above" on *Chromatica*. Elton describes Gaga as his family and she is even godmother to his two kids.

"THE EDGE OF GLORY"

Just when you think *Born This Way* is about to fade out with maybe a few ballads or filler, Gaga drops "The Edge of Glory" on you. One of the greatest closing tracks on any pop album, it's the ultimate mix of uplifting fist-pump ("Alright! Alright!") and racing dance music beats. But because Gaga never does what you expect, here comes a lengthy saxophone solo. Gaga called the song "Springsteenesque" and had one of Bruce Springsteen's band play the sax.

EMMYS

Gaga EGOT (Emmy, Grammy, Oscar and Tony Awards) watch: Gaga has four Emmy nominations but no win yet. She was nominated for her TV special for The Monster Ball Tour, two of her TV specials with Tony Bennett, and for her Super Bowl halftime performance. Even if she wins an Emmy in the future, she'll have to win a Tony award for a performance in a Broadway show to reach the EGOT alongside Audrey Hepburn and Viola Davis.

FAME MONSTER

With a run of hit singles and hardly any slow moments, Gaga's 2008 debut album *The Fame* was a big statement: although there were bubblegum pop moments like "Eh, Eh (Nothing Else I Can Say)," it was mostly harder-edged clubby pop. Unlike the flirty innuendo of other popstars, like Katy Perry or Britney, Gaga was more explicit, while still being fun: "LoveGame" rhymed "dick" with "disco stick." Music critic Brittany Spanos has called the album's title a "self-fulfilling prophecy"—when Gaga wrote these songs about being famous, no one knew her name... yet.

In a twist of 2008 fate, *The Fame* was held off the top of the US Billboard album chart by Susan Boyle from *Britain's Got Talent*. It did spend over 330 weeks on the chart, extended for an extra 74 weeks by Gaga's next move: in 2009, a deluxe version of the album came out. Deluxe versions of CDs were usually cash grabs with a duff extra song or two. But *The Fame Monster* was almost a whole new album with eight new songs, including "Bad Romance" and "Telephone." It was even nominated for Grammy Album of the Year in its own right.

F IS ALSO FOR...

FASHION!

There are three Lady Gaga songs with the word "fashion" in the title: "Fashion of His Love," "Fashion," and "Fashion!" The second of these was recorded by reality TV star Heidi Montag, but Gaga went ahead and released her own version for the movie *Confessions of a Shopaholic*. Later, "Fashion!" appeared on the album *Artpop*. The *Guardian* said it was easy to hear "Gaga's penchant for David Bowie in her tremendous, gliding vocal."

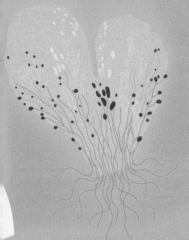

FERNS

A genus of ferns, Gaga, has been named after Lady Gaga. (Genus is the category one step-up from species, so horses and zebras are species in the genus Equus, for example.) According to scientists, the ferns, found in Central and South America, Mexico, Arizona, and Texas, have "somewhat fluid definitions of gender." In addition, their DNA sequence includes GAGA.

FAME PERFUME

Despite Gaga's hope that her first perfume, a unisex scent called "Fame," would smell like "blood and semen," in the end it was a more conventional mix of honey, saffron, apricots, orchid, and jasmine. In the bottle the perfume looked black, but became clear when you sprayed it. The promotional poster said the quiet part out loud about why people buy fragrance: a giant Gaga reclines naked while dozens of tiny men climb all over her body.

FRIENDS REUNION

Gaga popped up on the 2021 *Friends* reunion, dressed as a 1990s hippie chick with a fringed coat and acoustic guitar. Phoebe, played by Lisa Kudrow, started playing her song "Smelly Cat," one of the most famous and nostalgic elements of the show after "we were on a break". Gaga sings a slightly over-the-top rendition with a gospel choir and Phoebe mutters, "I still think it's better with just me." Gaga thanks her for being "the person for all of us on *Friends* that was—I don't know if this is the right way to say it but—the 'different one.'" Phoebe then thanks Gaga for carrying on the tradition.

FIBROMYALGIA

In 2017, Gaga tweeted that she suffers from fibromyalgia, a condition that affects the nervous system and causes horrible pain and fatigue. Somehow, Gaga has managed to keep up her career while suffering this, although the severity of her illness has forced her to cancel concert dates. She has said, "for me, and I think for many others, it's really a cyclone of anxiety, depression, PTSD, trauma, and panic disorder, all of which sends the nervous system into overdrive."

F IS ALSO FOR...

FLORENCE WELCH

Ethereal British singer Florence, of Florence + the Machine, appeared on the song "Hey Girl" on the *Joanne* album. Although the sentiment is about women supporting each other, the song doesn't quite hit the highs of some of Gaga's other collaborations. Gaga chose Florence because "her voice is sensational—she's one of the greatest singers in the world." Their friendship sounds really cute. In Gaga's words, "...we laugh a lot, there's a lot of hugging and being sweet to one another. She's just a sweet girl."

IS FOR

GAGA: FIVE FOOT TWO

In 2017, Gaga released a behind-the-scenes documentary entitled *Gaga: Five Foot Two*, her height in bare feet. This is not just another popstar documentary, unless you've seen other films where a singer conducts a strategy meeting topless.

There are incredible highs: watching Gaga being cast in a movie directed by Bradley Cooper that will one day be known as *A Star Is Born* is inspiring, especially when watching with the knowledge that this film will bring her an Oscar nomination. The lows are brutal, however, and we see Gaga sobbing in pain as she tries to recover from a past injury where she broke her hip. It's so severe that it interrupts the dance rehearsals she desperately needs to ensure her Super Bowl halftime show is perfect. The pressures of fame, the heartbreak of loneliness, and the anxiety of how *Joanne*, her most personal album to date, will be received have an obvious effect on Gaga. But, although she indulges in a "little baby meltdown" on the set of *American Horror Story*, she is consistently kind to her team and patient with her fans.

G is also for...
GRAMMYS

Lady Gaga has been nominated for 36 Grammys. Starting out with a single nomination for Best Dance Recording for "Just Dance" in 2009, she has now won 13 awards across nine categories. However, the "Big 4" of Album of the Year, Song of the Year, Record of the Year, and Best New Artist have evaded her. She's come close: *The Fame*, *The Fame Monster*, *Born This Way*, and *Love for Sale* have all been nominated for best album.

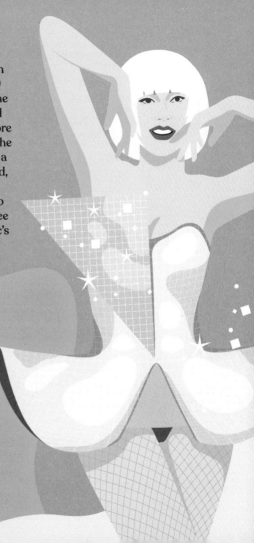

GLASTONBURY

For decades, Glastonbury was known mostly for its rock acts, but in 2009 a mirrorball alien touched down on the festival's Other Stage. Gaga changed costumes four times, which is four more than most festival acts. She also told the crowd she knows how it feels to be at a festival show: "...you're covered in mud, you're sweaty, and you're drunk." Accurate! Every year, Gaga's return to Glasto is rumored, but we are yet to see her on the main Pyramid Stage, music's most revered space.

GOSSIP GIRL

Gaga provided the inspiration for an episode of *Gossip Girl* (the original 2000s version, obviously) called "The Last Days of Disco Stick." The gang puts on a musical, very loosely inspired by Gaga songs, during which lonely boy Dan Humphrey gets dumped by Hilary Duff via "LoveGame" lyrics. In a show of her clout, Blair Waldorf arranges for the theater club to watch Gaga rehearse a performance of "Bad Romance."

IS FOR

HALFTIME SHOW

The crowd at the 51st annual Super Bowl must have been confused as to where the singing was coming from. Lady Gaga wasn't on the field, so where was she? Standing on the edge of the stadium's roof, singing Woodie Guthrie's people's anthem "This Land is Your Land." Behind her, hundreds of drones with red, white, and blue lights swirled and then formed the American flag. All of a sudden, Gaga leaped from the roof and ziplined down to the stage.

Performing mostly high-energy hits, with one emotional interlude for the ballad "Million Reasons," Gaga's performance was a wow moment. The support shown for LGBTQ+ people in "Born This Way" was beamed to a live audience of 117.5 million people. To date, a further 78 million have watched the show on YouTube. As she shouted out "Super Bowl 51" and threw down her mic, someone tossed Gaga a football and she leaped to catch it, falling out of sight below the stage. Quarterback Gaga caught the ball in steady hands but admitted she was nervous because "four out of five times that we practised it, I didn't get it."

H IS ALSO FOR...

HOUSE OF GUCCI

In *House of Gucci*, Gaga played Patrizia Reggiani, an ambitious woman who married into the Gucci family. Wearing real Gucci outfits from the 1980s, Gaga kept up the authenticity by speaking in an Italian accent for nine months while filming. "I never broke. I stayed with her," Gaga told *Vogue*. However, she was wary of meeting the real Patrizia as she felt "...this woman wanted to be glorified for this murder."

HOLD MY HAND

Unlike most sequels to beloved movies, 2022's *Top Gun: Maverick* was widely liked, not least for its music. The score was produced by Gaga along with legendary movie composer Hans Zimmer, who has tugged your heartstrings in everything, from *The Lion King* to David Attenborough nature documentaries. Gaga also wrote and sang a huge power ballad, "Hold My Hand," for which she was nominated for an Oscar. This brings her total number of Oscar nominations to four: three Best Song nominations in 2016, 2019 and 2023, as well as Best Actress in 2019 for *A Star Is Born*.

HAUS LABS

Gaga and her creative team launched a vegan makeup brand, Haus Labs, in 2019. Gaga called the products a "glamour attack" for "people that love to explore the artist within themselves and see themselves as a canvas." The brand was a huge success: by 2020, it was the third biggest-selling celebrity makeup line, behind only Rihanna and Kylie Jenner. A big overhaul in 2022 removed thousands of ingredients that Gaga described as "dirty," accompanied by a cleaner rebrand.

HAUS OF GAGA

Gaga's creative team, Haus of Gaga, creates her outfits and props. Although all popstars have a "glam" team (hair and makeup), creative directors, and costumiers, Gaga has given her collaborators more credit than most for making her vision come to life. In the liner notes for her first album, *The Fame*, she thanked 11 members of the team, including Matt "Dada" Williams. Among the countless costumes they have created for Gaga is the mirrorball "disco bra" that defined the club-kid look of her early career.

HILARY CLINTON

Gaga supported Hilary Clinton's presidential campaign of 2016. She performed at a Clinton rally, and gave an impassioned speech encouraging people to vote for her against Donald Trump, saying, "I could never have fathomed that I would experience in my lifetime that a woman would become president of the United States." After Clinton's defeat, Gaga protested outside of Trump Tower with a sign reading "Love Trumps Hate," condemning the new president's "angry, divisive approach to campaigning."

H IS ALSO FOR...

HAIR BOW

In 2008, Gaga appeared on the
show *Good Day New York* to
do one of those awkward
showcases where a popstar
has to perform their heart
out in a TV studio before a
man in a suit says, "and now
for the weather." On this day,
Gaga debuted the hair bow (as in,
a bow made of hair). She says "[The team] all f****** died,
we died. It never cost a penny, and it looked so brilliant."
In a reference to her past self, Gaga's 2019 Met Gala look
included tiny hair bows perched across her head.

IS FOR

INAUGURATION

In 2021, Gaga was invited to provide the centerpiece performance at the inauguration of President Joe Biden: singing the national anthem. She had previously shown her support for the Democrat candidate, singing and giving a speech at one of his rallies. Well, she wasn't going to vote for Donald Trump, was she?

As well as delivering a powerful vocal performance, her look told its own story. Gaga told *Vogue* magazine that the red and black gown, embellished with a bird brooch, was a highlight of her life in fashion: "One of my favorite things I've ever worn." Her hair was braided and she had a gold microphone to match the brooch, which resulted in comparisons to *The Hunger Games* online.

Deciding what to wear on such a huge stage meant choosing between a lot of dresses, but she said, "When I saw that golden dove, I just knew that this was the right piece, and I knew Schiaparelli, being an Italian fashion house, it was something that I really, really wanted to do for my heritage as an Italian-American woman."

I IS ALSO FOR...

INFLUENCE

Each year, the *TIME* magazine list of
the 100 most influential people
acknowledges those in the public eye
who are shaping the world we live in.
Gaga has been named on the list twice,
in 2010 and 2019. Fellow singer Celine
Dion wrote about Gaga for her 2019
inclusion: "She marched to the beat
of her own drum, knowing that her
message of individuality was a way
to express her inner strength. . . she
empowers her fans to adopt the
very same values in their lives—to
stand up for what they believe in,
despite what others might think."

IRIS VAN HERPEN

Dutch haute couture fashion designer Iris Van Herpen is an influential and experimental visionary who Gaga has worn many times. The most memorable outfit might be the multicolored look she wore to the 2020 MTV Video Music Awards, complete with a pink custom "gas mask." It featured Van Herpen's signature laser-cut spines, making Gaga look like a mysterious creature that had crawled up from the depths of the sea.

ISABELLA BLOW

In 2011, Gaga wrote in *V* magazine about the fashion icons of her youth: "I would dream of being a rock star who dressed like Mark Bolan, walked like Jerry Hall, and had the panache of Ginger from *Casino* and the mystery of Isabella Blow." British journalist Blow was renowned for her quirky style, which included a huge array of beautiful and surreal hats. When Gaga guest-edited *V* magazine in 2016, she created 16 individual covers, one of which was a picture of Blow.

IRON MAIDEN

A heavy metal band might not seem like the most obvious inspiration for a singer who alternates between high-energy pop and jazz standards, but Gaga cites Iron Maiden as an inspiration. After watching a gig in 2011, she said, "The devotion of the fans moving in unison, pumping their fists, watching the show, when I see that, I see the paradigm for my future and the relationship I want to have with my fans." Could "Heavy Metal Lover" on *Born This Way* be an Iron Maiden tribute?

49

J

IS FOR

JOANNE

Gaga's 2016 album *Joanne* was a big change in direction and caused controversy by not being at all controversial. Her inspiration was her aunt, who died at age 19. The album may be named after Joanne but aside from the title track it mostly explores Gaga's own relationships. She told *People* magazine: "My father was always very angry. He drank because of his sister's death. I was trying to understand him through making this record, and in that, also trying to understand why I love men that are cowboys."

Joanne was also an effort to broaden Gaga's fanbase: "I really wanted to reach that girl in the crowd who's got a kid in her hand and two kids running around her and a glass of beer in the other." Of course, we downloaded it enough to make it number one, but we were mostly confused at this stripped-back version of Gaga and missed the exuberant electro-dirtiness of her earlier music. *Joanne* makes more sense now we've seen *A Star Is Born*, which also carries a message that in order to get serious, you have to start playing rock.

J IS ALSO FOR...
"JUST DANCE"

Lady Gaga announced her existence to the world in 2008 with her first single "Just Dance," with iconic shoutouts to the producer RedOne, songwriter Akon, and of course herself, Gaagaaa. The song is about going out and getting drunk. It spoke to the hot mess girls and gays of the era in a way nothing had before, and after months of Gaga and guest singer Colby O'Donis performing on the club circuit, it finally climbed to number one on the Billboard 100.

JOKER

Gaga stars as the comic book anti-heroine Harley
Quinn in the movie *Joker: Folie à Deux*. The character
has also been played by Margot Robbie in *Suicide
Squad* and *Birds of Prey*. Gaga's Joker is Joaquin
Phoenix, and as both actors are known to use "the
method"—an intense process where you stay in
character all the time—the results could be explosive.
Not least because this version of the twisted love story
is a musical.

"JUDAS"

The video for "Judas," a single from *Born This
Way*, shows the apostles as a biker gang, and
Gaga caught up in a love triangle between Jesus
and his betrayer Judas. The clip includes biblical
references such as the washing of Jesus's feet and
being stoned to death as a sinful woman. Far from
being just to stoke controversy, the song and
video draw on Gaga's own faith. Norman Reedus,
who played Judas, said: "Gaga is super Catholic,
and gets everyone together for a prayer before
everything she does."

KERMIT COAT

Gaga's association with the Muppets is a long and respectful one that goes back to 2009. Even before she collaborated with them on her Thanksgiving special, she wore Kermit's likeness in the form of a coat made entirely out of Kermit the frogs, and created by Moroccan fashion designer Jean-Charles de Castelbajac. He also dressed Gaga in a floor-length black dress with feathers that nearly covered her face, and created the plunging, black-and-white, vinyl-look dress for the "Telephone" video.

Entertainment Weekly said they would be "interested to hear PETA [People for the Ethical Treatment of Animal]'s take on this faux frog get-up." Their wish was granted: the organization called it "genius" and quoted Gaga saying, "I hate fur and I don't wear fur." They were very disappointed in the following year's meat dress.

Ten years on from the creation of the piece, the designer posted a throwback picture of Gaga in the Kermit look, proclaiming "IRONY IS A WEAPON".

K IS ALSO FOR...

KATY PERRY

When popstar Kesha filed sexual assault claims against producer Dr Luke, Lady Gaga became involved when texts between the two women were leaked. In them, Kesha described Katy Perry as "mean" for not coming forward with her own allegations. Wisely, Gaga and Perry refused to let the media paint them as feuding, which would have distracted everyone from Kesha's case. Gaga said: "[Katy and I] have grown up in the industry together. We've gone through both celebrations & differences w/each other. These are old texts. We've matured, gotten over the past, love each other & share deep respect." Perry replied: "Love you too friend".

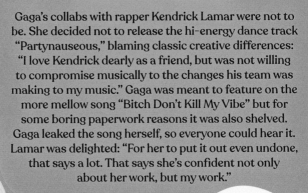

KENDRICK LAMAR

Gaga's collabs with rapper Kendrick Lamar were not to be. She decided not to release the hi-energy dance track "Partynauseous," blaming classic creative differences: "I love Kendrick dearly as a friend, but was not willing to compromise musically to the changes his team was making to my music." Gaga was meant to feature on the more mellow song "Bitch Don't Kill My Vibe" but for some boring paperwork reasons it was also shelved. Gaga leaked the song herself, so everyone could hear it. Lamar was delighted: "For her to put it out even undone, that says a lot. That says she's confident not only about her work, but my work."

KINDNESS

Gaga's belief in kindness comes from a deep place. She says, "I believe kindness is a human right... but it must be equal to all and especially sensitive to those who've been disempowered by their circumstances." Gaga understands what it is like to feel powerless. In an essay for the book *Channel Kindness* she describes the pain of being bullied at school and how she believes it stemmed from an absence of kindness.

L IS FOR

LOVE FOR SALE

Gaga's second album with her friend Tony Bennett, *Love for Sale*, came along in September 2021. It's a love letter to the songwriter Cole Porter, who had a wicked way with innuendo. Gaga brings out the naughtiness in the title track, which is about a streetwalker.

She sounds more relaxed and playful than on their previous collaboration *Cheek to Cheek*, in 2014. They are both obviously having a lot of fun, which is made extra-special by knowing that Bennett had been diagnosed with Alzheimer's disease. If most Gaga albums sound like a sweaty Saturday night out in the club, *Love for Sale* sounds like a lazy Sunday morning.

Love for Sale made Bennett the oldest person to release a new album, a Guinness world record. He also broke another record as the oldest person to be nominated for one of the major Grammy awards, when the collab was nominated for Album of the Year. Gaga had proved that she could sing jazz, and in 2023 she brought her solo jazz show to Vegas.

LADY STARLIGHT

Before Gaga became famous, she was hanging out at the bar where her boyfriend, Lüc Carl, was the manager. She met a dancer there called Lady Starlight and they were soon creative collaborators and best friends, starting bands and getting citations for public indecency together. Starlight says, "It was a magical connection—we were inseparable from the start." She DJ'd before every Gaga tour up until The Artpop Ball and is now a successful techno DJ.

LITTLE MONSTERS

The Lady Gaga fandom has a birthday: May 9th. That's the day in 2009 that she used the name "Little Monsters" to describe her fans for the very first time, while onstage in California. Most popstars now have a fandom name, but Gaga was the first Western popstar to do it, taking inspiration from K-pop.

THE LADY AND THE LEGEND

If you are a fan of Jazz Gaga, or cute inter-generational friendships generally, you'll want to watch *The Lady and the Legend*, a behind-the-scenes documentary about her last live show with Tony Bennett.

LETTERS TO A YOUNG POET

Gaga's favorite book is *Letters to a Young Poet*, a collection of poetry by Austrian writer Rainer Maria Rilke. She says she reads from it every day. She even has a tattoo on her arm of words by Rilke, which translate into English as: "Confess to yourself in the deepest hour of the night whether you would have to die if you were forbidden to write. Dig deep into your heart, where the answer spreads its roots in your being, and ask yourself solemnly, Must I write?"

LETTERS
TO
A YOUNG
POET

IS
FOR

MEAT DRESS

The MTV Video Music Awards have seen some of the most iconic and shocking outfits in all of pop history. Think Lil' Kim's purple jumpsuit that required a matching sparkly nipple cover, or Britney's olive green bikini, complete with a live python, for her 2001 performance. In 2010, Gaga topped them all when she arrived at the awards in a dress, boots, hat, and purse all made of real meat.

Gaga credits makeup artist Val Garland with the idea for the outfit, saying she "shared a story with me where she had gone to a party wearing sausages!" The dress is more robust than it looks: the shreds of meat were sewn onto a corseted base. Gaga's devoted stylist Brandon Maxwell nobly helped to sew meat onto the dress despite being vegan. The dress was preserved using taxidermy and is now in the museum of the Rock 'n' Roll Hall of Fame and *Time* named it the top fashion statement of 2010.

Gaga later revealed to Ellen DeGeneres that the outfit was a protest against the treatment of gay soldiers in the US Army.

M IS ALSO FOR...

MACHETE KILLS

Gaga's very first movie role in 2013 was as—what else?—a glamorous, shape-shifting assassin. She is up against a brothel owner, played by Sofia Vergara, in a race to kill the hero. Her character, La Camaleón (The Chameleon), can morph into anyone, which echoes how many times Gaga has changed her look in real life. Although she's only on screen for a few minutes, she manages to squeeze in a car chase and a costume change, from a red bustier into a yellow bustier.

MARK RONSON

Half-producer, half-celebrity, Mark Ronson has helped bring various albums to life, including Amy Winehouse's *Back to Black* and the Barbie soundtrack (his job is just "produce"). He produced *Joanne*, and he and Gaga also wrote "Shallow" together. Male record producers aren't renowned for their easygoing and respectful natures, but Gaga says that "[with] so many men in my life—in business and also that I've dated over the years—I just started to feel like what I was on my own wasn't good enough. And I don't feel that way working with Mark."

MICHAEL POLANSKY

Gaga went Instagram official with her boyfriend Michael Polansky in February 2020. Polansky runs a foundation started by Facebook cofounder Sean Parker. Parker is a good friend to Gaga—he introduced her to both Polansky and Bradley Cooper! Gaga hasn't said much about her partner in public except that "My dogs and the man that I love are my whole life."

MARY JANE HOLLAND

Many popstars have alter egos to help express themselves, like Beyoncé's Sasha Fierce or David Bowie's Ziggy Stardust. Gaga has had several, including her male alter ego Jo Calderone and her (theatrical gasp) brunette persona Mary Jane Holland. According to Gaga, she was recording in Amsterdam when she decided to dye her hair brown for a night out incognito: "I wanna have a good time, and I don't want anyone to know it's me I just need one night of just freedom—and I don't wanna be wearing another f****** wig while I'm doing it."

MADONNA

Madonna has always "expressed herself" when it comes to Gaga: she described "Born This Way" as "reductive" and "a blatant rip-off" of her own music. Gaga complained that "Telling me that you think I'm a piece of s*** through the media is like, it's like a guy passing me a note through his friend." Madonna has since insisted she has no grievance with Gaga and for her part Gaga seems keen to patch it up. She looked thrilled in a picture Madonna posted of them hanging out at the 2019 Oscars, with Gaga's statue for Best Song clutched in her hand.

M IS ALSO FOR...

MCQUEEN DRESS

Gaga has called Alexander McQueen "the greatest designer of all time." She wore a McQueen gown, with a long train and golden feather headdress, to the MTV Video Music Awards in 2010 (before changing into the meat dress). The outfit was a meeting of art and pop before *Artpop*: the swirly patterns are actually sections of paintings and sculptures by artists such as Hieronymous Bosch. Gaga says the dress is the "number one" look of her career.

IS
FOR

NOTES ON CAMP

The 2019 Met Gala theme was a minefield for certain celebrities. If you're merely beautiful and good at acting, you may not be well placed to interpret Susan Sontag's 1964 essay "Notes on 'Camp.'" But guess who was! Gaga, of course, naturally understood that camp is about spectacle and excess, done with a knowing wink.

She arrived in a billowing, room-sized, hot-pink Brandon Maxwell number. Dancers held black umbrellas over her—indoors. But then, the oversized coat was removed to reveal a black strapless gown with a bustle. Gaga deigned to carry her own umbrella at this point. This dress also came off and underneath was a pink satin sheath dress, accessorized with a 1980s brick phone and massive rhinestone sunglasses. Gaga applied lipstick, before stripping down to sparkly bra, underpants, and pantyhose.

US *Vogue* editor and fashion empress Anna Wintour is rumored to have said that if you tried to arrive after Gaga on the red carpet, you may as well "Just go home."

NYU

Gaga studied at the Tisch School of the Arts at the prestigious NYU. She dropped out after two years and so didn't graduate, although the school proudly lists her as an alumna. Gaga said, "I loved NYU, but I thought I could teach myself about art better than the school could. I really felt New York was my teacher and that I needed to bite the bullet and go it alone." She added with a touch of sass, "I wasn't interested in going to frat parties."

NO PANTS

Throughout the 2000s, skirts had gotten shorter and shorter, so it was natural they would eventually vanish altogether. Gaga defined the early 2010s look by dressing in bodysuits, or underpants and bra tops. She told *Rolling Stone* magazine in 2009 that "I feel freer in underwear, and I hate f****** pants." This wasn't a passing phase: although she favors gowns on the red carpet, Gaga still walks around LA without trousers on in her downtime.

N IS ALSO FOR...

NATIONAL EQUALITY MARCH

Gaga is known for her activism, but there was something special about her appearance at the National Equality March back in 2009. It came as no surprise that she spoke out in 2019 against Donald Trump, when he was in office. But Gaga also insisted Barack Obama follow through on his pledge to legalize same-sex marriage and provide other freedoms. "Obama, I know that you're listening. Are you listening? We will continue to push you and your administration to bring your words of promise to a reality."

IS
FOR

OSCARS NIGHT

Gaga's performance at the 2015 Oscars ceremony was hotly anticipated. Everyone wanted to know what elaborate, wacky outfit she would wear or what stunt she'd pull onstage. Subverting expectations completely, Gaga arrived in a gorgeous white Alaïa couture gown.

She had been working with a vocal coach every day, to achieve the technical skill needed to match musicals legend Julie Andrews, for a special performance of songs from *The Sound of Music*—and she nailed it. Gaga told Billboard:

"The truth is, you can either nail a performance like that or butcher some of the most classic songs sung by an all-time great. I took the gamble because everyone had written me off."

Gaga has become the jewel in the crown of the Oscars ceremony, returning in 2016 to sing "Til It Happens To You." Her duet with Bradley Cooper, singing "Shallow" in 2019, set the internet on fire with reactions to their incredible chemistry. "Shallow" won Best Song, although Gaga missed out on the award for Best Actress.

O IS ALSO FOR...

ONE LAST TIME

Gaga's friend, the late Tony Bennett, who was one of her most important collaborators, turned 95 on August 3rd, 2021. To celebrate the veteran singer in the most appropriate way, he and Gaga put on a special concert with full orchestra. The One Last Time concert was a tongue-in-cheek reference to Bennett's age, as it was finally time for him to retire after more than 70 years. Like the professional he was, he gives it his all despite being physically frail, and Gaga is obviously having a blast performing with her friend of many years, and the man she described as her "musical companion."

OREOS

One of the all-time best pieces of pop music merch, bar none, was the Chromatica Oreo cookie. Wrapped in metallic pink foil rather than the familiar blue, the cookies themselves had pink dough and an emerald-green filling. Each one was stamped with a simplified version of the *Chromatica* cover, a heart to celebrate "Stupid Love," or simply the word "Chromatica."

ONE WORLD: TOGETHER AT HOME

Remember the global pandemic and how the days blurred into one and you didn't feel like doing anything? Lady Gaga cannot relate. She organized an online fundraising concert to make money for the World Health Organization, with performances from celebrities like J-Lo, The Rolling Stones, and Taylor Swift. Gaga said she was thinking of "all of you that are at home who are wondering when this is going to be different" and sang the classic song "Smile," composed by movie star Charlie Chaplin in 1936.

OPRAH INTERVIEW

Gaga was invited onstage as part of Oprah Winfrey's 2020 Vision Tour, a series of interviews and wellness talks. As part of their in-depth, vulnerable chat about physical and mental health, Gaga opened up about the bullying she endured at school, as well as her PTSD from sexual assault as a teenager. Oprah asked Gaga how she kept going after all this trauma? Gaga paused, pointed to the audience, then to Oprah, and said, "women like you."

ORDAINED MINISTER

On July 24th, 2011, gay marriage was legally recognized in the state of New York. Lady Gaga had the bright idea of becoming an ordained minister, so she could help gay friends and fans achieve their dream of marriage. The Universal Life Church accepted Gaga's request to become a minister and she was able to ordain the marriage of her friend and yoga instructor Tricia. As a minister, Gaga can technically request to be called Reverend Gaga.

O IS ALSO FOR...

ONE DIRECTION

At the MTV Video Music Awards in 2013, at the height of their fame, One Direction won an award. They bounced up to receive their award for Best Song of the Summer for pop anthem "Best Song Ever" and for some reason the crowd started booing. Remember 2013, when it was cool to sneer at music that girls like? Gaga was caught on camera looking back at the crowd and shaking her head in disbelief. She later went backstage and told the 1D boys: "I just want to tell you that you deserve every bit of success that you have and don't you dare let those people boo you." You can't get a much better endorsement than from a certified Queen of Pop!

P IS FOR

"PAPARAZZI"

A single performance changed pop and put Lady Gaga right at the top of the new pop-girl hierarchy. Gaga won three awards at the 2009 MTV Video Music Awards, the same number as Beyoncé. These days, an infamous interrupted speech involving Taylor Swift tends to be what people remember from the night, but in any other year, Gaga's jaw-dropping rendition of "Paparazzi" would have made the headlines.

Even when you know what's coming, it can make you gasp. Set against an ornate villa backdrop, Gaga appears in pure white. Her voice sounds on point, especially when she takes to the piano, with one foot up on the keyboard like a mix of Mozart and Weird Barbie. The tone flips from smooth vocal runs to a hoarse scream as Gaga staggers to centre stage, blood pouring from inside her top as if she's been stabbed. The backdrop suddenly looks like a reference to Shakespeare, as if Gaga is trapped in a tragic plot. We end with Gaga dangling above the stage, a spotlight fixed on her bloodied face. It is stunning, unbelievable. Gaga is confirmed as a genius.

P IS ALSO FOR...

POLAROID

There's something both sleazy and arty about a polaroid photo, so who better to represent the camera company than 2010 Gaga? Taking on one of her earliest creative collabs, Gaga said, "I am so excited to extend myself behind the scenes as a designer, and as my father puts it, finally have a real job." Haus of Gaga came up with the "Polaroid grey label" line, which included a Bluetooth polaroid printer that could be connected to your phone.

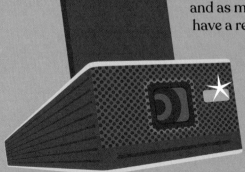

PRESS TOURS

Actors sometimes seem to hate doing press for movies. Not our Gaga. As Louis Staples wrote in *Vulture* magazine, "If there were an Oscar for Best Actress in a Promoting Role, Gaga would have surely won for *A Star Is Born*." To Gaga, the chance to answer the same question about her motivation 20 times in a row is just another stage on which to shine. Sometimes, her press tour performance is a better movie than the movie itself: on the *House of Gucci* press tour we learned that "if I weren't who I am today, I would have been a combat journalist." Picture that.

POLICE TAPE

When Gaga is trapped in her cell in the video for "Telephone," she wears an outfit made of black-and-yellow crime-scene tape. A bespoke creation by designer Brian Lichtenberg, it is fantastically camp but also has a serious message. The tape reads, "CRIME SCENE DO NOT ENTER" and could be interpreted as a reference to Gaga's status as a survivor of sexual violence.

QU ER AL Y

When Lady Gaga accepted a MuchMusic award in 2009, she thanked "God and the gays" and an icon was born. Gaga is loved and claimed by the queer community for her flamboyance and talent, but also for her steadfast public support and activism. Earlier in her career, Gaga said that "Poker Face" was inspired by her bisexuality. Recently, she has described herself more as a supporter and ally, leading to some confusion and scepticism from people who want to see her dating both men and women as some kind of "proof."

It's ultimately no one else's business how Lady Gaga identifies. One thing we can be absolutely sure of is that Gaga stands up for the LGBTQ+ community more than almost any other celebrity. She's donated money to homeless queer youth, and spoken up against homophobic violence. She was even threatened with arrest and a $50,000 fine in Russia for allegedly "promoting homosexual propaganda" in 2012. She took to the stage in Moscow shouting "Cuff me, Russia, arrest me! I don't give a f***!"

QUEEN ELIZABETH II

When Gaga met the Queen of England, she wore a bright red latex dress with huge puffed sleeves and glitter patches around her eyes. To be clear, that's what Gaga wore, not Queen Elizabeth II. The monarch wore a glittery black gown and shawl to attend 2009's Royal Variety Performance, where she met Gaga and watched her perform "Speechless." Gaga said, "I wanted to dress like a queen in a British fashion and I also wanted to do it in my way."

"QUICKSAND"

A song that didn't make the final lineup for *The Fame* found its forever home with Britney Spears. "Quicksand" was included as a bonus track on European editions of her *Circus* album. The song sounds exactly like 2008 Gaga, with speak-singing similar to "Poker Face." Gaga and Britney have been public about how much they admire each other. Speaking about the end of Britney's conservatorship, Gaga said, "she is wildly talented. She is incredibly inspirational... And, she authored her freedom."

QUEEN OF POP

As soon as she came on the scene, critics began referring to Gaga as the new queen of pop. In 2011, *Rolling Stone* magazine named her the queen in its rankings, just beating Rihanna and Taylor Swift. Up until then, this royal status had always been given to Madonna. Gaga and Madonna are both queens because they serve hits, but also understand that to be truly great, you must create an iconic visual identity.

IS

FOR

"RAIN ON ME"

The second single from *Chromatica* dropped at both the worst and best possible moment: "Rain on Me" came out in May 2020. There wasn't a lot of new music available in 2020, let alone pop. Three queens emerged to save the first months of lockdown and rescue us, at least in our imaginations, from the endlessly bleak landscape of boredom balanced with fear for our lives. Dua Lipa's album *Future Nostalgia* was the soundtrack to the earliest days of exercising in your living room, and just when we'd listened to that perhaps 50 times, Gaga and Ariana Grande stormed in with "Rain on Me."

When you listen to the lyrics, the song is about surviving pain and trauma, but it could have been about unicycling and we wouldn't have cared, as long as it had a thumping beat and an uplifting sound. Illustrated by a cyberpunk-inspired video, which had dancing and ended with the two pop goddesses hugging, the song was a mainstay of many pandemic playlists, reminding us that the dancefloor would one day open again.

R IS ALSO FOR...

RED LACE

After stunning the crowd with her performance at the 2009 MTV Video Music Awards (VMAs), Gaga stepped onstage to accept an award. She won Best New Artist for "Poker Face." To accept the moon-man statuette, she wore an Alexander McQueen dress made of blood-red lace. Gaga said, "it was meant to be a continuation of the VMA performance. So after the princess had been murdered by the paparazzi, the red lace was meant to symbolize sort of my eternal martyrdom." Gaga's team added a red crown to complete the "queen of hell" look.

THE ROLLING STONES

Rock band The Rolling Stones were a surprise collaborator of Gaga's in 2023. They dropped a single, "Sweet Sounds of Heaven," along with the legendary performer Stevie Wonder, in September 2023. Where did all these people meet and decide to record a song together? Gaga made a surprise guest appearance at the band's *Hackney Diamonds* album launch, held at a small club in New York. She and Mick Jagger had a vocal battle to see who could bring the most intense, bluesy quality to their half of the duet, almost screaming into their mics.

REPEAL DON'T ASK DON'T TELL

An important cause in Gaga's ongoing support for LGBTQ+ people was getting rid of the policy of "Don't Ask Don't Tell," which required queer people serving in the US military to remain closeted in their professional life or lose their jobs. In September 2010, Gaga spoke at a rally in Maine, where activists were lobbying senators to break the gridlocked vote to repeal. She said, "I'm here because 'Don't Ask, Don't Tell' is wrong, it's unjust and fundamentally it is against all we stand for as Americans." The tireless efforts of many queer activists worked, and a year later the discriminatory policy was repealed.

RED ONE

If RedOne was remembered for nothing other than Gaga's weirdly catchy rendition of his name at the beginning of "Just Dance," he would have a place in the pop history books. But as the producer for 14 songs from Gaga's first three albums, from "Poker Face" to "Bad Romance" to "Judas," we can thank him for helping to create that quintessential early Gaga sound that perfectly combines pop maximalism with a dark twist. In 2015, RedOne (real name Nadir Khayat) started a record label and now works for FIFA, the international football association.

A STAR IS BORN

By 2018, Gaga had achieved enough success in music to make her famous forever. But when the movie *A Star Is Born* came out that year, she proved that she had more than one world-class talent. Bradley Cooper's directorial debut tells the story of troubled musician, Jackson Maine, who meets Ally (played by Lady Gaga) when he sees her singing in a bar. United by their love of creativity, they are instantly drawn to each other, and quickly fall in love. Ally goes on tour with Jackson, and for a while it seems like a fairytale. But his demons never go away, and while Ally becomes more and more famous, Jackson spirals down into darkness.

The movie was a smash hit and instant classic, turning Gaga and Cooper into permanent A-list Hollywood stars. Critics and fans praised Gaga for her committed performance, and for playing against type with an unglamorous look—at least to start with. Gaga described the portrayal as "a very, very strong expression of what it means to become a star... Ally does not really become one until the last frame of the movie."

SIN CITY: A DAME TO KILL FOR

Gaga was made for the drama of black-and-white movies. She had a short cameo in Robert Rodriguez's 2014 movie *Sin City: A Dame To Kill For*—even shorter than her appearance in his other movie *Machete Kills*. She plays a waitress who takes pity on Joseph Gordon-Levitt's character and her attitude and huge, piercing eyes steal the scene. As great as her cameo was, it was time for Gaga to become the leading lady: her next movie was *A Star Is Born*.

SO YOU THINK YOU CAN DANCE

Gaga appeared as a judge on the 2011 series of *So You Think You Can Dance*. Gaga always takes art seriously and always gives 120 percent of what is required. Wearing a mermaid-y green wig and Versace outfit, she gave feedback that was just as heartfelt as the dancers' performances. She cried while saying: "there were so, so many things wrong that I did when I was younger and so many things I wish I could take back, and I felt every moment of that through your dance tonight."

THE SOPRANOS

Gaga's very first acting role was as "Girl at Swimming Pool #2" in the TV show *The Sopranos*. The show, about mafia boss Tony Soprano, is famous for its writing, but Gaga's character is just there to laugh at the antics of teenage boys messing about in the pool. Nevertheless, she learned from the experience: "When I look back on that scene I can see exactly what I did wrong... I didn't know how to listen."

S IS ALSO FOR...

SATURDAY NIGHT LIVE

New York's famous live sketch show has invited Gaga to perform and act many times. Her first appearance, in 2009, included a fake fight with Madonna in a sketch about competing pop divas. In 2011, she appeared in a sketch called "The Golden Rule" about a threesome. In 2023, she dropped in to introduce host and musical guest Bad Bunny, a Gaga fan who says he listens to *Chromatica* "when he feels sad."

"SHALLOW"

The song that won Gaga her first Oscar is a love duet. It's unusual, though, as it starts with Bradley Cooper as Jackson Maine seeming to question whether we need modern technology. It builds into a power ballad, and Gaga bursts into an impassioned chorus about letting go and diving into the waters (of vulnerability). In a key scene of *A Star Is Born*, Jackon and Ally write the song together, testing the waters of how to join together creatively and romantically. The song, written by Gaga and Mark Ronson, has become a karaoke staple.

"STUPID LOVE"

The first single from *Chromatica* was exactly what Gaga fans had been waiting for: a blast of happy, upbeat pop. Although Gaga is incredibly smart, this song is about the joy of having no thoughts, risking it all to open up and fall in love, and also dance around in a pink wig. It was the first time Gaga had ever worked with super-producer Max Martin, who created tracks for songs like "...Baby One More Time" for Britney and "Shake it Off" for Taylor Swift. Together they made "Stupid Love" a huge comeback to pop for Gaga after her triumph with the soundtrack to *A Star Is Born*.

I'M WITH STUPID

CAN'T DANCE

BAD ATTITUDE

FOUR EYES

T IS FOR BROWN EYES

CAN'T SING

THEATRICALITY

Whatever anyone may say now about it being cheesy, when *Glee* was in its prime, it was the freshest show on TV. It had a diverse cast and a dark sense of humor, and it took pop music seriously. In 2010, the overlap between people who liked Gaga and people who watched *Glee* was basically 100 percent. So it made sense that they dedicated an episode from the bonkers first season to her. "Theatricality" featured the club dressing up in outfits, including the bubble dress, to sing "Bad Romance." Rachel Berry, played by Lea Michele, finds her long-lost mother Shelby, played by Idina Menzel, and they sing a yearning acoustic version of "Poker Face."

In season two, the club learns about self-acceptance through a performance of "Born This Way". Each character wears a white T-shirt with their biggest insecurity written on it to learn to embrace them. A highlight of the episode is ditsy cheerleader Brittany trying to help her partner Santana accept being a lesbian, but accidentally making her a T-shirt saying "Lebanese".

THERE CAN BE A HUNDRED PEOPLE IN A ROOM

"There can be a hundred people in a room and 99 of them don't believe in you, but all it takes is one and it just changes your whole life," Gaga said on the *A Star Is Born* press tour, on day one. And day two, three, four... This lovely statement about how Bradley Cooper believed in her enough to cast her as his co-star in his passion project quickly caught on as a meme. Gaga revealed that the source of the quote came all the way from her childhood vocal coach Don Lawrence, who said it to her when she doubted she would ever make it as a singer.

TONY BENNETT

Gaga's collaborator and mentor, the late Tony Bennett, was born in New York in 1926, and rose to be one of the most popular singers of the 1950s, eventually selling 60 million records. As befits a close friend of Gaga's, he was passionate about equality and became involved in the civil rights movement in the 1960s, going on marches, and singing at benefits. His obituary in the *New York Times* said, "With the possible exception of his former wives, everyone, it seemed, loved Tony Bennett."

T IS ALSO FOR...
TEACUP

Who remembers the teacup era? In 2009, Gaga started carrying around a purple and gold teacup. According to Gaga, she wanted to see if she could turn a teacup into a celebrity: "I wanted to say something on a real level about fame. I decided to take a purple teacup out of my collection and take it to London and make it famous."

T IS ALSO FOR...

"TIL IT HAPPENS TO YOU"

If you've never seen Gaga's performance of "Til It Happens To You" at the 2016 Oscars, put this book down and go and watch it now. She is absolutely singing her heart out, channeling her own experience of violence. Toward the end, the backdrop rises and dozens of women who survived sexual assault take to the stage. When the song, which featured in the 2015 documentary film *The Hunting Ground*, was nominated for an Oscar, Gaga wrote, "Myself and Diane [Warren, co-songwriter] are simply honored to represent the voices of so many survivors."

TRANS RIGHTS

Gaga never forgets to support the "T" in LGBTQ+. When she kicked off her Vegas residency in 2023, she had something on her mind. "I've got something to say about trans rights in this country," she said, and then the opening chords of "Born This Way," from her indelible equality anthem, rang out. She had already made her stance clear in a speech at New York Pride back in 2019, when she said: "...while we have made tremendous progress, we find ourselves at a time where attacks on the trans community are on an increasing rise each day. I will not tolerate this."

TAYLOR KINNEY

Gaga met the actor Taylor Kinney on the set of the music video for "Yoü and I." They got engaged on Valentine's Day in 2015, and appeared nude on the cover of *V* magazine in 2016, but split later that year. They seem to have remained amicable: in her *Gaga: Five Foot Two* documentary, Gaga gets flowers from Kinney to congratulate her on her Super Bowl performance. However, she also notes that she "did a movie" and lost him, hinting that her success may have been a factor in their separation.

IS FOR

UNPLUGGED

The *MTV Unplugged* series is famous for letting artists show off their vocals in intimate, acoustic settings. Iconic episodes include Mariah Carey and Nirvana, and in 2021 it was time for Lady Gaga and her beloved creative partner Tony Bennett to show what they could do vocally.

Although she is dressed in a demure 1950s-style gown in seafoam green, Gaga does not take her performance down a notch just to match the stripped-back music. Playing songs from *Love For Sale*, Gaga brings frenetic, Tina Turner-esque energy to the stage. Tony keeps it cool as ever, letting Gaga handle the banter. She steps in to help the older artist as he seems to tire, letting her take over for a rendition of "Let's Do It." To close out their set, Gaga asks if he'll sing his signature song, "Fly Me To the Moon." Although he is struggling to speak, Tony sings a note-perfect version, while Gaga sits on the stage, watching him with tears in her eyes. Tony sings the final line—"I love you"—to his wife in the audience. He brings the house down.

U IS ALSO FOR...

URCHIN
OUTFIT

When Gaga went on a night
out to a club in 2014, instead of
putting on jeans and a nice top,
she wore a giant, inflatable,
glitter-effect, sea urchin costume.
Designed by British artist and fashion designer Jack
Irving, the outfit had two dozen spines. When Gaga
stepped out of the car, they hung gently around her
like a jellyfish, but then in front of the waiting paparazzi,
she inflated the spines so they stood up, rising to several
meters above her head.

UNFINISHED TRILOGY

There's a fan theory that the videos for "Paparazzi" and "Telephone" have a secret third instalment, creating a trilogy that tells an entire story. Both videos have a murder-revenge plot against men who scorned the female singers. In "Paparazzi", this means poisoning Gaga's boyfriend, while in "Telephone" it's Beyoncé's boyfriend and an entire diner of people, who are poisoned. The video for "Telephone" does end on the tantalizing words "to be continued." Whether this was teasing the third in a poison trilogy or a third Gaga/Beyoncé collab (Gaga also appeared on her song "Videophone") we may never know.

UNICORN TATTOO

Gaga has 24 tattoos on her body, ranging from a rose with the words "La Vie en Rose" around it (a reference to the Edith Piaf song she sings in *A Star Is Born*) to a big unicorn holding a banner saying "Born This Way" on her thigh. The unicorn might be the ultimate Gaga tattoo. She says, "The unicorn is born magical and it's not the unicorn's fault and it doesn't make it any more or less special or any less unique." If anyone was born magical, it's Gaga.

UNIVERSITY

Gaga attended New York University's Tisch School of the Arts and made the most of her time at the highly regarded performing arts school. Gaga's classmate Carly Waddell remembered how "there was a piano, and she would sit at the piano every single day and just play and sing *Wicked* at the top of her lungs." She added: "You can't argue, that girl is really good". Gaga was only 17 when she arrived and eventually dropped out to pursue fame, a bad plan, but one that clearly worked out for her.

VEGAS

When Gaga agreed to do a Vegas residency, how could she please the distinct fanbases that loved either her dance-pop persona or her jazz persona? Gaga refused to choose: her solution was to plan and execute not one but two entire shows. Beginning in 2018, she alternated two different shows with a very different look and sound. Enigma was a pure pop spectacle, incorporating mirrorball costumes, choreography, impassioned piano playing, and all the other signature Gaga codes. The setlist included all the songs fans hoped to hear, from "Bad Romance" to "Beautiful, Dirty, Rich."

For her second show, Jazz & Piano, Gaga combined classic tunes like "Anything Goes" with jazzy arrangements of hits like "Poker Face" and "Born This Way." As soon as pandemic precautions allowed, Gaga resumed Jazz & Piano and has been performing exclusive, limited runs of the show ever since. The residency has been a smash hit—audiences love it, and Gaga apparently gets paid over $1 million per performance.

A VERY GAGA THANKSGIVING

In 2011, Gaga recorded a Thanksgiving TV special at her old school, the Convent of the Sacred Heart. The gothic building is the perfect setting for an intimate concert, mixing classics such as "White Christmas" with high-energy hits like "Born This Way." The tone is sugary sweet: she even crafts with third and fourth graders and chats about their favorite Thanksgiving foods. In 2013, she followed up with the hundred times more chaotic, and much more fun, *Lady Gaga and The Muppets Holiday Spectacular*

VOCALS

Lady Gaga has a mezzo-soprano vocal range. This means she has a lower range than a soprano, the sort of singer who can hit high, operatic notes. This is perfect for belting out pop songs or jazz standards. As well as being able to sing across three octaves, Gaga has power in her voice and, of course, plenty of passion. These all add up to a stunning singing voice that makes Gaga one of the greatest vocalists in the world.

VIDEO PORTRAITS

The experimental artist Robert Wilson designed the set for Gaga's performance of "Applause" at the 2013 MTV Video Music Awards (a landscape of white paper cutouts). He then asked if she'd like to appear in his ongoing series of video portraits. Gaga and Wilson recreated a painting by the artist Ingres, with Gaga standing so still she seems like a painting herself. But suddenly she closes her eyes. Wilson described Gaga as "serious—not your ordinary pop star." His four video portraits of Gaga were displayed in the Louvre museum in Paris.

V IS ALSO FOR...

VERSACE

Gaga has a long-standing relationship with the fashion house of Versace. She appeared in an advert for the brand in 2013, presumably snapped up after Donatella Versace, the head designer, heard "Donatella" from the *Artpop* album. Gaga said in 2014, "Seeing where Donatella is and how far she's come and continues to go makes me feel like I have a role model." Gaga has worn Versace on the red carpet many times, including to the 2023 Academy Awards, where she wore a dress just four days after it had appeared on the runway at the Versace fashion show. Gaga also released a line of accessories with Versace to raise money for her Born This Way Foundation. A 360-degree collaboration!

IS FOR

WITCH

Following her leading lady turn in *American Horror Story: Hotel*, Gaga made time for a cameo appearance in *Roanake*, in the following season. The story focuses on a haunted house in North Carolina, where the mysterious lost colony of Roanoke settled in the 16th century. Every year in October, the ghosts of these long-dead colonizers are able to pass through the veil and enact horrible murder on the house's occupants. Gaga's character, a Scottish witch called Scáthach who narrowly avoided being burned at the stake, is the source of the ghosts' immortality. As is typical in *American Horror Story*, her plot revolves around a combination of terrifying supernatural powers and weird sexual situations. The witch's affair with the man of the house leads directly to at least two grisly deaths.

Hilariously, Gaga herself was accused of being a witch and practising Satanism after taking the stage at a Biden rally. Right-wing conspiracy theorists claimed she'd been a part of Satanic rituals to discredit her.

W IS ALSO FOR...

WAXWORKS

Like all popular celebrities, Gaga has been honored with several waxworks, some more accurate than others. Waxworks are a fun opportunity to have your photo taken with your fave singer, or at least a slightly melted version of them. In 2010, the famous Madame Tussauds waxwork museum launched eight brand-new Gagas in branches around the world. The Gagas included her David Bowie tribute look and Gaga dressed as a Christmas tree.

WINE

Gaga has collaborated with the fancy champagne brand Dom Pérignon to create several vintages of sparkling wine. The collectors' items come in a Gaga-themed box and include a fizzy pink rosé version, which sells for around $400. Gaga says she has a sentimental attachment to the brand as "I actually used to always drink Dom Pérignon with Tony Bennett." As with many of her collabs, profits go to Gaga's Born This Way Foundation.

WORLD RECORDS

As befits a global superstar, Gaga holds a number of world records. According to the Guinness World Records, she has the fastest-selling digital album in US history, moving an incredible 662,000 digital copies of *Born This Way* in a single week in 2011. She was also the first person ever to be nominated for Best Actress and Best Original Song at the Oscars, for *A Star Is Born* and "Shallow" in 2019. By the end of 2020, four of her songs ("Just Dance," "Pokerface," "Bad Romance," and "Shallow") had sold 10 million-plus copies worldwide, a record for a female artist.

X

IS

FOR

X BEYONCÉ

Beyoncé has been one of Gaga's most important collaborators. They are both queens of pop, two of the very few women who have been able to consistently fill stadiums for their live tours. They also both have powerful and devoted fandoms and are true artists as well as celebrities.

Their first collaboration was on Bey's song "Video Phone", elevated from virtually nothing by a video stuffed with exceptional looks on both ladies, including matching white bodysuits. Gaga told MTV, "I have never laughed so hard on a video set in my life. We had the best time doing 'Video Phone'." The behind-the-scenes video confirms their gigglefest. Gaga clearly adores Bey and calls their friendship the "real woman alliance." Their duet on "Telephone" followed, with Bey and Gaga playing Thelma and Louise-style friends on the run, obviously complete with iconic outfits. They may be operating at the same level, but the pair refuse to be put head to head in the race for queen of pop. Of Gaga, Beyoncé says: "Lady Gaga might be the sweetest, sweetest angel ever."

X IS ALSO FOR...

X VALENTINO

Gaga has worn Valentino many times, including a long, periwinkle-blue gown to the 2019 Golden Globes while she was promoting *A Star Is Born*. She is also the face of the fashion brand's perfume Voce Vita. The brand's head designer chose her because she "represents ambition, dreams, strong will." The advert for the scent featured Gaga's duet with Elton John, "Sine From Above."

X ARIANA GRANDE

Gaga seems to get on well with other popstars, and Ariana Grande is no exception—the ponytailed one added her airy vocals to "Rain on Me." Gaga says she feels protective of Ari like a popstar big sister: "It was this beautiful, I think very healing process for me, not necessarily having a female artist that mentored me as I came up." Ari agreed, saying that "she immediately felt like a sister to me." The collab is a fan favorite and won the Grammy for Best Pop Performance in 2021.

X MUPPETS

Only true icons collaborate with the most important found family in all of entertainment, the Muppets. Gaga's 2013 TV special *Lady Gaga and the Muppets Holiday Spectacular* features a chemistry-laden version of "Baby It's Cold Outside", with actor Joseph Gordon-Levitt, only slightly marred by Gaga being unable to dance in her long, red dress. An impassioned version of "Gypsy" with Kermit led to rumors in the press. Gaga laughed: "I hope Miss Piggy's still not mad about Kermit. We're just friends!"

"YOÜ AND I"

One of Gaga's best power ballads— "Yoü and I"—is also one of her most vulnerable songs. From her second studio album, *Born This Way*, the song goes into personal detail about her relationship with bartender Lüc Carl, her pre-fame boyfriend of six years. The clue is in the ü, but there are also references to a guy from Nebraska, where Lüc is from.

The video features Gaga as a mermaid, singing in a cornfield and a barn, and a cameo by her male alter ego, Jo Calderone.

"Yoü and I" has a rocky, almost country sound, that reflects Lüc's taste in music, which is more rootsy than Gaga's usual pop: the lyrics reference him singing "Heart of Gold" by rock artist Neil Young to her on her birthday. The song also samples "We Will Rock You" by Queen. It's a warm portrait of someone Gaga says she has "written a lot of music about." Filming the video for "Yoü and I" brought an added bonus: after casting gorgeous actor Taylor Kinney as her love interest, Gaga went on to date him.

YELLOW DIAMOND

For the 2019 Oscars red carpet, Gaga wore a piece of jewelry so beautiful, and with such a unique history, that it is priceless. The huge yellow diamond, hanging from a necklace of white diamonds, is over 100 years old. The last woman to wear the jewel was Audrey Hepburn when she was promoting her role in the classic movie *Breakfast at Tiffany's*. Gaga's Oscars look referenced Audrey's: a black silk dress worn with long black gloves.

YASS GAGA

Gaga is part of many key moments in fan and internet culture, culminating in the unscripted moment credited with mainstreaming the word "yass." If you are reading from the future, this was a slang term originating in queer culture that meant "I strongly approve!" Gaga was leaving a hotel in 2013, when fan Mikiel Benyamin shouted "yass Gaga you look so good!" The video was uploaded to the social media platform then known as Twitter and went viral.

YELLOW HAIR

Gaga is known for being blonde, but on occasion she has pushed the shade right into the primary colors. In the video for "Telephone," she wears a wig with yellow ends, in keeping with the bold, pop-art look of the clip. On the red carpet at the 2010 Grammys, she showed up in a cellophane-effect Armani dress with matching star object, but the real star moment was her unnaturally bright yellow hair. As blondeness is almost synonymous with female pop-stardom, the yellow hair feels like a commentary on Gaga's usual blonde hair.

Y IS ALSO FOR...

YOKO ONO AWARD

Every other year, the famous experimental artist Yoko Ono gives a prize to people who raise their voice to work for peace. Recipients have ranged from the political activist and artist Ai Weiwei to the nation of Iceland. In 2012, she awarded the prize to Lady Gaga, along with other recipients such as the Russian protest group Pussy Riot. The award came with a $50,000 grant, which Gaga donated to the Elton John AIDS Foundation.

ZIGGY STARDUST

David Bowie, with his gender-fluid presentation and genius-level visual imagery, has been a major influence on 21st-century popstars. In particular, the glamorous stage persona he came up with, Ziggy Stardust, has inspired artists to take their performances and image to greater heights.

Lady Gaga counts Bowie as one of her idols. She even has a tattoo of his *Aladdin Sane* album cover, which shows him with a lightning bolt painted across his face. She called it "the image that changed my life," and in her earliest days of fame was often seen with a lightning bolt painted on her face.

At the 2016 Grammys, Gaga paired her bright blue outfit with a bright red wig, designed to look like Ziggy Stardust's red hair. She performed a medley of Bowie's hits at the ceremony to honor her hero, who had died just a few weeks earlier. A lightning bolt in changing colors was projected onto her face as she sat at the piano. Later, an emotional Gaga said, "I feel like my whole career is a tribute to David Bowie."

Z IS ALSO FOR...
ZIPLINE

Gaga is no stranger to aerial acrobatics—let's not forget her high-wire leap to the stage for her Super Bowl half-time performance. Back in 2011, a slightly less dramatic zipline carried her around 100ft (30m) across Central Park while singing "Bad Romance." The *Good Morning America* concert series had put on a Gaga show for the public. She sang five songs, playing a keyboard attached to a black-and-purple glitter-horned unicorn.

ZANE LOWE

Journalist Zane Lowe is known for his long-format interviews with musicians. Speaking about *Chromatica* in their 2020 interview, Gaga told him: "I've been open about the fact that I have had masochistic tendencies that are not healthy. They're ways of expressing shame. They're ways of expressing feeling not good enough, but actually they're not effective. They just make you feel worse." She went on to discuss the power of starting a new album, and how she sees each one as a new beginning. She sees this "new beginning" as a place from which she can both heal herself and, hopefully, inspire others.

ZODIAC

Stefani Germanotta was born on March 28th, 1986, right in the middle of a Mercury retrograde, a time in the calendar that is famous for bad luck and chaos. Her zodiac sign is Aries, which means she is outgoing, adventurous, and bold, perfect for a popstar, who needs to make risky moves and shine bright. Her Scorpio moon sign means she is also good at speaking about the hidden, taboo areas of life.

ZEDD

The German DJ and producer Zedd (remember his massive song "The Middle"?) has worked on several Gaga songs. He remixed "Born This Way" and "Marry the Night" for *Born This Way: the Remix Album*. The good working relationship continued with Zedd providing heavy dance beats for "G.U.Y.," "Aura," and "Donatella" from *Artpop*.

AUTHOR SATU HÄMEENAHO-FOX

Satu is a writer and editor from London. A pop culture fan and theorist, she has written books on celebrities, fashion history, and nature. You can find her either in a museum gift shop or tending to her orchard.

ILLUSTRATOR NASTKA DRABOT

Nastka Drabot is an illustrator based in Warsaw, Poland. Her love for contrasting colours and an architectural background influenced her illustration style. An architect must perform as a straight line —be precise and reliable—and this is the best definition for her vectors.

QUOTES & REFERENCES

2: "Gaga Gone Wild", *Out* (out.com). **5:** "Lady Gaga: 'I Missed the Applause So Much'", *SiriusXM* (youtube.com). "A chaotic journey through ARTPOP", *Mike's Mic* (youtube.com). **6:** "Lady Gags mentor - Top 4 American Idol 2011", *Paul fromMN* (youtube.com). "American Idol 2011: Lady Gaga mentors", *The Washington Post* (washingtonpost. com). **7:** "Gaga just bought those McQueen Armadillo boots", *Dazed* (dazeddigital.com). "Lady Gaga gushes over House of Gucci co-star Adam Driver...", *Daily Mail* (dailymail.co.uk). "Adam Driver addresses Lady Gaga sex scene...", *New York Post* (nypost.com). **8:** "Lady Gaga Is Born Again", *Elle* (elle.com). **12:** "Lady Gaga - Monster Ball: Brave Speech", *mich97* (youtube.com). "Andy Backstage - Saturday Night Live", *Saturday Night Live* (youtube. com). "How Lady Gaga's bubble-blowing dress was created", *Dezeen* (youtube.com). **27:** "Lady Gaga says she stayed incubated in Grammy 'vessel' for 72 hours", *Entertainment Weekly* (ew.com). "Lady Gaga Says She 'Was in the Egg for Three Days' Before 2011 Grammys", *Vanity Fair* (vanityfair.com). **28:** "More than a friend, @ladygaga is family to me...", *@eltonjohn* (twitter.com). **29:** "Google Goes Gaga...", *Talks at Google* (youtube.com). **33:** "Nineteen species of fern named for Lady Gaga", *Duke Today* (today.duke.edu). "Lady Gaga's New Fragrance Will Smell Like Honey, Vanish in Midair", *The Cut* (thecut.com). **34:** "Lady Gaga & Lisa Kudrow Sing 'Smelly Cat' on Friends Reunion", *Saiq* (youtube.com). "Lady Gaga on her fight with fibromyalgia: 'Chronic pain is no joke'", *Global News* (globalnews.ca). **35:** "Lady Gaga about her friend Florence Welch", *Gaga Shorts* (youtube.com). **42:** "It's Not An Imitation, It's A Becoming...", *British Vogue* (vogue.co.uk). **43:** "Lady Gaga On The Power Of Make-Up...", *British Vogue* (vogue.co.uk). **44:** "Lady Gaga Protests Outside of Trump Tower After Hillary Clinton Loses Election", *The Hollywood Reporter* (hollywoodreporter.com). "Lady Gaga addresses screaming crowds at Hillary Clinton rally in North Carolina", *BBC News* (bbc.co.uk). **45:** "Growing Up Gaga", *New York Times* (nymag.com). **47:** "Lady Gaga On

The Meat Dress and 19 Other Iconic Looks", *British Vogue* (youtube.com). "Lady Gaga Recalls Wearing Dove Brooch at Joe Biden's Inauguration...", *People* (people.com) **48:** "Lady Gaga by Celine Dion", *Time 100* (time.com). **49:** "Lady Gaga: 'Iron Maiden changed my life'", *NME* (nme.com). "V99 Gaga's Fashion Guard", *V Magazine* (shop.vmagazine.com). **51:** "'I Love Men That Are Cowboys': Lady Gaga Talks Writing 'Joanna'...", *People* (people.com). **53:** "Lady Gaga answers religious blogger over claims about Catholic celebrities", *Independent* (independent.co.uk). **55:** "Lady Gaga covers Kermit the Frog... all over her body", *Entertainment Weekly* (ew.com). "Lady Gaga Wears Coat Made of Kermits", *PETA* (peta.org). "IRONY IS A WEAPON...", @jcdecastelbajac (instagram.com). **56:** "Lady Gaga Breaks Her Silence on Leaked Texts...", *Variety* (variety.com). **57:** "Kendrick Lamar and Lady Gaga's Partynauseous leaked online", *Guardian* (theguardian.com). "Kendrick Lamar says Lady Gaga is 'a beautiful person' with a 'genius mind'", *NME* (nme.com). "Lady Gaga on surviving lockdown...", *Irish Independent* (independent.ie). **60:** "DJ: 'I was Lady Gaga's mentor'", *Digital Spy* (web.archive.org). **63:** "Lady Gaga On The Meat Dress and 19 Other Iconic Looks", *British Vogue* (youtube.com). "Lady Gaga Speaks About Meat Dress On Ellen", HYnews (HYnews.com). **65:** "11 Things We Learned in Lady Gaga's 'Five Foot Two' Netflix Documentary", *Billboard* (billboard.com). **66:** "Track-By-Track ARTPOP Commentary by Lady Gaga", *ARTPOP Jesus* (web.archive.org). "Madonna Says Lady Gaga is 'Reductive'", *ABC News* (youtube.com). "Madonna Puts Lady Gaga Feud to Bed With 'Bloody Mary' TikTok", *Paper Magazine* (papermag.com). **67:** "73 Questions With Lady Gaga", *Vogue* (youtube.com). **69:** "Lady Gaga perfectly captured 'camp' at the Met Gala by paying homage to drag culture", *GQ* (gq-magazine.co.uk). **70:** "Lady Gaga Ditched NYU to Study the Art of Fame", *MTV* (mtv.com). "Lady Gaga Worships Queen and Refuses to Wear Pants", *Rolling Stone* (rollingstone.com). **71:** "National Equality March Rally: Lady Gaga speaks", *Inside, Looking Out* (youtube.com). **80:** "Lady Gaga to become Polaroid's creative director", *Guardian* (theguardian.com). **81:** "No One Does a Press Tour Quite Like Lady Gaga", *Vulture* (vulture.com). "It's Not An Imitation, It's A Becoming...", *British Vogue* (vogue.co.uk). **83:** "12 Times Lady Gaga Showed Love for the LGBTQ Community", *Billboard* (billboard.com). "Lady Gaga clarifies whether she 'represents' the LGBTQ community", *Attitude* (attitude.co.uk). **84:** "When Lady Gaga met the Queen...", *Metro* (metro.co.uk). "Britney Spears thanks Lady Gaga for her support: 'You're my inspiration'", *Today* (today.com). **88:** "Getting to Know Lady Gaga", *Oprah* (oprah.com). **89:** "Lady Gaga joins Maine rally for repeal of 'Don't Ask Don't Tell'", *Guardian* (theguardian.com). **92:** "Lady Gaga cries on So You Think You Can Dance", *On Demand Enter* (On Demand Enter.com). **93:** "Lady Gaga reflects on her *Sopranos* acting debut...", *Entertainment Weekly* (ew.com). **94:** "Bad Bunny discusses Lady Gaga and Chromatica", *D Todo* (youtube.com). **98:** "Lady Gaga Is Born Again", *Elle* (elle.com). "Tony Bennett, Jazzy Crooner of the American Songbook, Is Dead at 96", *The New York Times* (nytimes.com). **99:** "Lady Gaga explains teacup mystery", *Digital Spy* (digitalspy.com). **100:** "The nomination lends a voice to victims & survivors...", @ladygaga (instagram.com). **101:** "12 Times Lady Gaga Showed Love for the LGBTQ Community", *Billboard* (billboard.com). **105:** "The Special Meanings Behind All 24 of Lady Gaga's Tattoos", *Popsugar* (popsugar.co.uk). "Bachelor alum Carly Waddell reveals Lady Gaga drove her 'crazy' in college", *Independent* (independent.co.uk). **108:** "Robert Wilson's macabre video portraits of Lady Gaga", *Wallpaper* (wallpaper.com). **109:** "FASHION Magazine February 2014 Cover: Lady Gaga", *FASHION* (fashionmagazine.com). **115:** "Lady Gaga On Beyonce: 'She Is A Real, Real Woman'", *MTV* (mtv.com). "Lady Gaga on Beyonce's reaction to the 'Telephone' video..." *Entertainment Weekly* (ew.com). **116:** "Valentino's new fragrance is an ode to Lady Gaga", *Financial Times* (ft.com). **117:** "Lady Gaga and Ariana Grande Rain Down Excellence in 'Rain on Me' Video", *Vulture* (vulture.com). "Lady Gaga was 'too ashamed' to befriend Ariana Grande after their collab...", *Mail Online* (dailymail.co.uk). "Lady Gaga Teams Up With the Muppets and Adorable Photos Result", ABC News (abcnews.go.com). **119:** "Lady Gaga talks about Lüc Carl", YCHproductions (youtube.com). **120:** "'Yas queen': What it means and where it comes from", *PinkNews* (thepinknews.com). **123:** "Lady Gaga Channels David Bowie by Wearing an Orange Wig and a Blue Blazer...", *E News* (eonline.com). "Lady Gaga: 'My whole career is a tribute to David Bowie'", *NME* (nme.com). **125:** "Lady Gaga Talks Mental Health, Mentoring Ariana Grande and Making 'Chromatica'...", *Variety* (variety.com).

Editor Millie Acers
Designer Isabelle Merry
Senior Production Editor Marc Staples
Senior Production Controller Louise Minihane
Senior Acquisitions Editor Pete Jorgensen
Managing Art Editor Jo Connor
Managing Director Mark Searle

Written by Satu Hämeenaho-Fox
Cover and interior illustrations Nastka Drabot

DK would like to thank Caroline West
and Kath Stathers for proofreading.

First published in Great Britain in 2024 by
Dorling Kindersley Limited
DK, One Embassy Gardens, 8 Viaduct Gardens,
London SW11 7BW

The authorised representative in the EEA is
Dorling Kindersley Verlag GmbH. Arnulfstr. 124,
80636 Munich, Germany

A CIP catalogue record for this book
is available from the British Library.
ISBN 978-0-2416-7165-8

Printed and bound in China

www.dk.com

MIX
Paper | Supporting
responsible forestry
FSC™ C018179
www.fsc.org

This book was made with Forest
Stewardship Council™ certified
paper – one small step in DK's
commitment to a sustainable future.
**For more information go to
www.dk.com/our-green-pledge**